Invasives

Invasives

Poems by Brandon Krieg

Many Voices Project 129

First Edition
Library of Congress Control Number: 2013950945
ISBN: 978-0-89823-302-5
Many Voices Project Award 129

Cover and interior design by Morgan Leapaldt
Author photo by Colleen O'Brien

The publication of *Invasives* is made possible by the generous support of
The McKnight Foundation, the Dawson Family Endowment, the Lake Region
Arts Council, Northern Lights Library Network, and other contributors to
New Rivers Press.

For copyright permission, please contact Frederick T. Courtright at 570-839-7477
or permdude@eclipse.net.

New Rivers Press is a nonprofit literary press associated with
Minnesota State University Moorhead.

Alan Davis, Co-Director and Senior Editor
Suzzanne Kelley, Co-Director and Managing Editor
Wayne Gudmundson, Consultant
Allen Sheets, Art Director
Thom Tammaro, Poetry Editor
Kevin Carollo, MVP Poetry Coordinator

Publishing Interns:
David Binkard, Katelin Hansen, Jan Hough, Kjersti Maday, Richard N. Natale,
Emily Nelson, Joe Schneider, Daniel A. Shudlick, Lauren Stanislawski,
Michele F. Valenti

Invasives Book Team:
Jan Hough, Lauren Johnson, Hannah Kiges, Jonah Volheim

Printed in the USA

New Rivers Press books are distributed by Consortium Book Sales & Distribution

News River Press
c/o MSUM
1104 7th Avenue South
Moorhead, MN 56563
www.newriverspress.com

for Colleen

CONTENTS

I, Inc.

I incorporate gneiss and coal and
  long-threaded moss
  and fruits and grains
and esculent roots, a gravity dam
  550 feet high on this
  the continent's steepset
river machine, with 13 other dams, a system
  of locks and
ladders for commerce, continuance

of species, twin
cooling towers of a data-center
  for the world's most powerful
search engine, installed at the site of a lost
  Babel where first
  peoples converged
in that universal language: trade, night-spearing

of salmon by torchlight
  lost (men's faces aflash
  in archives), expressionist
  petroglyphs eerily
  contemporary, photographed
by professors before
  the big sink, I incorporate
with irrigation ditches, thousands
  of gridded miles
of piping, hoses, scaffolding for sprinklers,

insecticide banners
over alfalfa terraces greenshining to the edge
of the glacier-cut gorge,

and on the ridges:
white windmills, futurist
        crosses, revivalist
architecture of potato magnates, societies
        for the preservation of automatic, semi-automatic,
        Gun Hill, Gun River, without judgement —
that sucked candy — I incorporate

the leaden
        groundwater under
firing range and echoing
factory, the capful of phosphates,
        Chicago River run backward
        to Mississippi, algae clotting
the Gulf's left ventricle, plumes of oil filmed
        by unmanned cameras
        designed to sustain
unearthly pressure, ingenious inhibitors
        of serotonin reuptake
present from sewage in measurable amounts
        in the Great Lakes,
        and calm
as the not-I appears, I incorporate
the not-I,

the talkers
in headsets talking to no one present,
Bach and baseball and
      tobacco stocks ticking, the screen-lit
      lotuseating faces staring,
clicking — disgust me, and I incorporate them
      with the disappearing

bees, defense drones
undetectable except
      by ordnance flowering
      skull, sternum, uterus, I am born
      at many removes
from Thoreau, who paused to notice
      the thickness of surface ice,

and, tormented
by his still form in the hut doorway,
sun on skin, outside time, I incorporate it and it binds
      the mettle in my blood,
      the compound sinking
to my feet — impossibly heavy, I drive them

into mountains topped with blinking
towers, zigurrated by
      logging roads, in a motley
      of clearcuts and

necklaced with triple-stranded cables whose buzzing
sounds like rain, and up there
        walking the ancient

Cascade Volcanic Arc, I incorporate
the green company of grunts
        on leave in sunburned skulls, who go
        silent posing
on a high promontory — premonitions
        of Hindu Kush — they frighten me
        with politeness
on the trail, acne, and large vulnerable ears,
I could clap their shoulders, clasp them, pretend to

spar as with my brothers,
but, helpless to keep them
        for their families' sakes
        from disappearing
into the photograph's digital veil, can only
        incorporate them as I must
        these actors charging the hill
        on a screen in a window
I walk under later, many rooms are lit this way,
the allegory literalized, and I am outside

in another cave
of streetlights flicking on under cameras,
I pass through these and incorporate their recordings of me
        into that Gordian nerve-net

of me not recorded, firing
charges down too many
forks to be
reliably
modeled, the loops
of its feedback with external
stimuli so intricately in-nested, a representation

of them would curve its outer ring
through the Oort,
and I must go farther,
into imagined futures, incorporate
cornstalks 12 feet high with black leaves modified
by photosynthetic silicates for 90 percent effiency of capture
and acorn-sized kernels,
they are beautiful if not yet
realized, and I am afraid
of them, utterly, as I was in Chicago homesick

for Trask and Kilchis, Siletz and Nestucca, and found,
at the eastern end of Pratt Street where it abuts the lake,
frozen corpses of
chinook salmon

washed up like grotesques out of my memory —
transplants are everywhere, translations of
translations, no place embodies itself, all

overlap, and so I
incorporate them, unifying
them in one brand,
       Brandon, meaning
       from a flaming hill
as claimed by a bookmark given me when young —
       I place it in the book of grass
 and the book catches fire and illuminates
       the undersides of clouds,
       an advertisement
       like the orange GE
glowing on a building in Midtown
       seen by the lovers
       naked in infinite
       regress of two walls of hotel-room mirrors,

and, full disclosure: it was I positioned against her
       in the mirrors' smallest frame,
feeling I have lived in invisible abstract cornucopia diminishment
       of frame within frame where
only images propagate — invincible-distant
as the acronym haloes guarding Mannahatta's skyline —

corporations are all.

Resist or acquiesce; I incorporate
their paltry specializations into this brand
       whose acronym is every star in the night sky,

and in the day sky too,
　　　for though it is invisible, it is nevertheless
　　　present, totalizing, undemocratic
as every corporation aspires to be,

　　　and, reader far hence,
face lit by a little held charge, a little water's motion,
　　　a million-stranded rope of sand,
all of my swindling and evasion is for our certain merger,
　　　for I am corrupt as every other,
　　　and you must absorb my assets

as I have absorbed this
　　　broadcast image
from Stalin's Ukrainian famine — the infant automaton
　　　in the street still nursing on
　　　its starved dead mother.

Swallow me and go.
I do not wait for you I am in you already.
There is commerce between us.

Fallen Empire's Tiny Chemical Sun

Timberline reached,
I dig old snow
to heat on a tin
East German folding stove;
add jasmine tea —
Sunflower Brand,
Fujian Province —
to the pot; mark
the fuel disk's origin:
Chemische Fabrik
Westeregeln;
read the tea tin's
proclamation: People's
Republic; see far
Seattle in smog gone
sunset-molten;
savor the lees.

Discovery Park

You return from
        summer Iceland.
For nine weeks sun
        in sines skimmed

lupine horizons:
        to see so much
purple unsettles,
        you said, *it's*

unnatural-natural.
        We climb to bluffs,
sun slips mountains,
        your first dark

in months, first stars,
        first ferries silently
crossing the sound,
        first city rising

east—terribly
        luminous.

Astral Plaint

Lewis, long lulled on by the unearthly Pacific,
wept to find it violent: surging to obscure the stars.

Lincoln leveled a path through unbroken forest
for the telegraph, and no one could stop stars
from speaking Morse. Edison was frantic

to trap the buzz of his starry head in a filament,
then cities became constellations' mirrors.

Ford died conjuring a car that would survive
the journey back to childhood, over whose dark fields
Pisces still arced. Roosevelt decreed a dam

against the sky, and the Columbia swallowed
basalt petroglyphs of human heads emitting light.

Gates ran a creek through his cavernous living room,
flipped all of the switches and sat under dark screens,
listening to a lone salmon spread its starry milt.

Domus Aurea

Driving by Bonneville Dam's sublime
arches at night, I remember Rome.

On the Esquiline, in view of the Coliseum,
I asked a famous historian how it could be
no contemporary praised Nero's vision —
a palace overwhelming three hills
in the capitol of the world, that became
the world in miniature: bizarre beasts and slaves
from every land; confounding plants; a lake
to stage great naval battles, plays, masques;
mosaics and frescoes so surpassing natural
the Renaissance would lower itself
on ropes into the ruins to steal a glimpse;
spigots spuming floral scents; a mechanized
ceiling of constellations rotating like the sky . . .

"He couldn't keep art separate in his mind,"
was the answer. "Everything he touched transformed
to simulation, and many died to make it so.
He was hated. Except for a few descriptions —
terse — his palace is an ellipsis."

Above the turnout, Bonneville's floodlit arches,
wedged between dark hills, churn the current
into screens up and down this provincial coast.
I see, flickering later in windows
above The Dalles, faces before the screens —
rapt, avid — touching the keys repeatedly
changing their minds. There is no ceiling
to their constellations. Their eyes:
dots in an ellipsis.

Inversion between the Fish Counters at Bonneville Dam

I could count seven hundred salmon flashes in an hour
while watching in that falling wall of water
the triumph of Caesar, red as Capitoline Jupiter,

not long before he was murdered and deified. Some still leave,
it's said, flowers in the forum where his tomb is thought to be.
Never mind. I was a classics major home from the university

with a nervous disorder, was told a repetitive task
might take my mind off Rome's decline. I sat before a glass
viewing window and counted, in their spawning masks —

hooked-jawed, severe — male chinook returning.
Joe Garrison sat in the other folding chair, burning
as he said, his Indian half with a flask, and earning

nearly twice my wage for the more difficult-to-spot hens.
"What's your other half, Joe?" I asked. "Half salmon,"
he said, "what's yours?" I said: "Imperial Roman."

He laughed. "The best gladiators were Colville Indians," he said,
"They learned by spearing salmon to spear a man dead
at thirty yards, from a speeding El Camino's bed."

I laughed hard. Then wanting to reach him these words
formed by inversion before I could check them. We both heard:
"To kill a man, kill his salmon — that's what the Romans learned."

Note from the Romans

Punch eyeholes in your helmets
and be skulled messengers
      of death. A simple cage
is good to hold the most grotesque

creatures on display. Perfect the placement
of pebble-sized mosaic tiles
      and you will be kept

from growing finned tails and slipping
into irreversible water; you will build a bridge

high enough to make the sky
flow under it
      like a parade of prisoners.

Still, you may be awakened by a sound
of jugs pouring over stones.

The cages will be wet but empty,
the winds seem heated by the faraway

clapping of burst men's mouths
like cod-mouths grasping
      at strange light.

And if the same light
                    should seem to fall
from the bridge at night, making it shiver

in the forward ripples of the river,
cover, if you can,
                your lidless eyes.

Atlas Industries

This gravel path that starts among the town's poor
stove-door and car-part-strewn
backyards runs thirty-seven miles
to Haven. Sunday I pedaled past the sparsely

emptying churches, porches leaning
a little out of true, the odd
barn-backed farmhouse among the smaller
frame houses, the tavern with too-clever name

beside an abandoned gas station,
rows and rows of saplings still in white
plastic winter jackets, until a high ridge
eclipsed the clouds on my right, and I stopped

at a chain-gated road guarded
by this sign: Atlas Industries. No one in sight,
I leaned my bike, walked the gravel
to where the hill suddenly utterly plummeted

a clean-walled hundred feet
into little dull piles of itself. Bald
terror came over me then, of having stumbled
onto the stage of some remote amphitheater,

where strata of faces anticipate
the foreshadowed sacrificial bull or *deus ex machina.*
My role: the initiate into the cult of aggregate
that has long underwritten all his ways,

who walks to the stage's center, stands
before the blink-less dozer proffering its unpoured
pile to the sky, and sees how, from every place
now, unmoved, we move the earth.

Processed

I worked at the cannery before coming to this hatchery,
so you can forgive my fantasy

of breeding cylindrical fish without bones
or tails, or scales, or dorsal or adipose

fins — one roll of pink meat machines
could slice neatly to fit tin cans.

It is when I am injecting
smolts with tags computers at the dams will be detecting —

I start to think rather
than each tag transmitting its seven digit number

to a program predicting adult harvests three
years later, we could save money

by raising these process-ready salmon in holding tanks
without an ocean longing. I imagine the thanks

the governor will lavish on me as we stand
for our picture by the conveyor, at the plant

where I once worked,
watching the pink skinless disks of meat lock

into the waiting socket of each can
with satisfying precision. Then the governor hands

me one of the salmon my daydream has made
as cameras flash, and I see it has no eyes and become afraid.

Speck

My father appears, creased
to sell machines, whose ion beams
detect, on polished silicon disks,
defective circuit memory.

He opens his briefcase to show
a darkened salmon.
It's been polished so often
it has hardened like a totem.
It is stranger than Leviathan.
It is formed of our Lord Doubt.

When he is alone,
my father takes it out
and sets it on the hotel bed.
This proves to him he had a son
who shied from the insistence of the depths.

And the father took the creaking pole,
and pulled against the beast with jagged grin,
and shrapnel up and down its skin,
and bottles breaking up its belly,
whose slime is saccharine and scent of lilies,
whose nostrils blind its eyes with smoke,
who clacks like keyboards fin to finish,
whose half-life shames our hopes.

And our Lord Doubt spoke:
Behold: you cannot see him he is probable.
Behold: you cannot see him he is wave.
Lay thy approximation against him;
remember the battle.

My father tells me, *Haul this memory*
though every city
and stuff its mouth with votive money,
it has become too heavy.
But he is trapped inside of it
with me: an egg within an egg within an egg.

Inside, Lord,
I feel your speck of silicate.

Hinoki

Labial niche in an oak trunk.
    There were shrines
you said, *in a trunk, an old man wanted*
to die there, was forced

to live. Above us,
    the root-radii of another fallen
oak. *In Chicago*, I said, *I saw*
a Japanese cypress carved in the likeness

of a silicon mold
    made from an unnamed
fallen California
tree. You bend to capture this

impossible red
    clover with your phone,
send its image to Boston
where a botanist friend will know

its Latin name, but not what it is
    to inhabit such
lake-ward slanting red.
I think of the world of signals passing

through us always now,
          wind of abrading shrines
in which we must
live on past human time.

Outskirts

I discovered the very tire, perhaps, through which
the creek's Chinook were Styxed,
remembered them

jagged and terrible as
obsidian arrowheads, impossible
as basilisks, returning

to a paleolithic apprehension
those who came upon them
oceansized and violent in
all shallowness.

Gone as arrowheads ground to sand;
gone as myths whose mouths
stopped.

I refused to sit
with the difference, diminished; I got up

to follow inklings of purple lupine,
vanilla leaf, long fingers
of coral-root ringed by bees,
and leaned and breathed this sting

of sea-reek so unlike.

Through the scent's familiar arches, I ran
to the ridge's edge,
where the creek's revolving carves a kind of nave —
there beyond belief:

ten black Chinook picked to rags,
laid at diagonals in the slowness,
committing their ooze to air.

Above the dead
a clot of tiny smolts hovered,
each wearing its pulse like a thread

in a coat of many colors.

November

Childwise vision
of a coho thrashing in thin floodwater blankets
on a black road.

Enraged with milt, it slithers over asphalt.
It will not reach the redd;
it will not pass the code
that maps from source to mouth its fluent god.

Yet I return
to its struggle ditch-ward to spawn alone
on the sharp, damp rocks.

This is where I was born.

Conditions of Blood

Long before Joverape and virginbirth, the sea
rubbed fresh genitals against continents
climaxing in the mineral
conditions of
blood,

fell shivering back into clitoral cloud-hood:
lightning overloading its
synapses — proto-
bacterial

life!

Compulsion without remedy.

Falstaff Sifting Fish Trash

Fish cleaning station, Newport Bay, OR

Look at these shotten herrings dangling long ropes
down from the pier, each a dull child
waiting for his unspooled yo-yo to return,
each dreaming his sunken pot will come up
hissing with Dungeness —

Bait-brains! I piss on your pots' polite chicken livers!
Oh, you sunned a squeak of reek from them?
Two days on the fence post?
Crabs scramble to matter more noxious:
these gutted albacore at the trash bin's bottom
with eyes like smashed watch-faces, smelling thunderous.

Herringbones like a dry, scentless, picked-clean
neatness, and has a wife
with antiseptic smile who forms a smart display cake
of his sweet white claw-meat. After dinner he feels most man
being chewed up and spit out where she is toothless.
It's otherwise with me.
I was born with these blunt hard teeth to crack the very clamps
that pick at me in dreams. My agile tongue can feather
life out of the cracks. Who will say I'm not a lover?

Look at this gashed lingcod
making the face we are all about to make.
Crabs will place the bone crown on him and send him
turning deeper than moonlight reaches.

Herringbones cannot fathom the spectular waltzes
I dream, across death's wide drowned deck.
I have been promoted to Vice-Admiral,
and crabs cling to my massive flesh like medals.

The End of Metaphor

1.

This godawful clod of man
        with eyeglasses warped
as sea-relinquished bottleglass,

by which he tracks his blessed dog
where the surf shrinks, has turned
        and waits for me, his hand

juggling free of weed strands
        a thing he gives to me:
That's a rare find — angel wings!

which is a white mussel shell
opened, pinioned
            to him as

the terrible anomalies
shrieking down
heaven.

It crumbles in the hinge of my outstretched
mind.
They're usually broken up;

        find another if you're lucky.

2.

Picking through strangulated kelp,
I find the buried bulb
at coil's end.

Stretch the unreal length straight out —
        livid scourge!
                monstrous sperm!

O unlikeness.

Pick through
        the mossy beards stripped
from prophets, washed

ashore here — where
are your microbial lips, Pythagoras?
Pick apart green strands

and find the sand flea's throne:
a trail of bubbles going deeper,
                        my love says,

kissed by unlikeness.

3.

That angel-winged sand flea
Giordano Bruno,
          that mutation stricken,

no sandgrain glinting has yet
escaped his mnemonic,
                    who evaporated

at the stake, now beads
a hundredfold
on the oils

of a tern's lost under-down tuft:
image that has nothing to do
                         with Argus,

that watches over my life.

Fraught Stop on the Coast

Circle of crags,
crashing walls,
waving yarrow:

river cove
gated by
the highway's arches.

I go alone;
somewhere near
my love sulks,

pretends to sun.
I wear black,
shine, obsidian,

wrong among
sandstone shards
that line the walls.

From sandy pinholes
sand fleas vault
a surfperch skull;

I think on
the long coast road,
love — confusion

of endpoints, origins.

Sweet Delay

Cars on 1, a line around the headland
stopped. One lane blocked by landslide boulders
a sunburned crew picks at on the cliff.
In the unconditional air, on the bent guardrail,
I sit with the other drivers, watching fog-silks slip
over grass-slicked foothills, wave-sprays
explode from a gull-circled monolith of schist.
Screened by windows, we watched sea lick
the mountains' feet all day. Now, to smell its mists,
to sense its concussive pulse, seems obscene —
like entering pornography. The others hurry
into their cameras' viewfinders. One man
throws stones into the unmarkable blue-green.
My love bends to touch the tiny ice plant's leaves.

Standstill

Last night,
worst fight:
whole trip's
warped belts
just slipped
clean off.
Standstill.
Every coastal
mile marked,
we've arrived:
two teary
ditches drain
the whole
continental
plate. So,
what now?
I strip the hot
breath-filled tent
to mesh,
lie down
parallel
you — clenched
beneath the
claustrophobic
stars.

Clasp

At dawn, I emerge
alone — a sycamore,
wide-crowned, alone,
has scoured the shell-rim
sky of grit, has let
the day-moon into camp.
Whatever I have done,
this deer knit from neck
to flank with lightning pulses
calmly clouds with breath
the brush beside my table,
ambles off. I rise
to trace the understory
of this tree, sit by creek
and see — just as I feel
your hand upon my back —
the tiny clasp that opens
the morning glory.

Shilshole Bay

for A.W.

We find one intact
shell, like an icon
among shards,

and later, under a leaning tree,
wedged in shore boulders,
a hundred apples.

First bite: too ripe.
I toss the fruit against a stone;
it spits its star.

You say the Greeks lacked
our constellations —
Don Juan; Tristan, Isolde —

and love her, yet
other faces occur as flawless
shells to your fingers.

Married, I mull
my skull stuck in the niche
next to its icon.

We leave in agreement these
hundred apples
bobbing in saltwater.

Compass

Mussels cluster on black rocks like magnetic shavings.

God my compass
with many centers and no circumference,
I am lost

in you since I relinquished
sex my pole star —

the long, red needle-beaks pry
the black shells open

to thrill flesh, but you are love
without proof or precedent, therefore:

Love, Augustine

                        Down here!

love is usage.

Fishing Rock

Black monolith annealed of numberless obsidian dice
waiting to be worn free, rolled by wave fingers
without tally —

moon wins —

aloof in remote gravity, yet formed
of the same force

that melded these billion particulars
into an awe-shape:

disks of pumice   black dice

no bones   all vaporized

no delicate inlines to suggest the muscular outlines
that once shot through sea like a shower of arrows —

sun the archer —

only a gray tufa-like slab crowning the black rock:
spolia of an empire, fossil-less
as the moon.

The sun stops first at its altar.

Levels

Every pit high in the cliff's terraces lives
on the sea's excesses —
sculpins, anemones, small crabs the color of stone

shift and twitch in shallow cragpools,
unaware worlds
upon worlds enfold their stratospheres of foam:

star-freaked domes, bald thrall moons
that sway
disturbances in remote elements:

the tidal jets and sprays, for instance,
refreshing these
oases of gill and claw that also fill the dead

crabs' littered, piked-clean
headpieces
with reflections of such wide

miniscule skies.

Combers

In my enthusiasm for crag-crashing
waves that jet up and suspend —
spectral chandeliers — then
collapse clearfire,

I found a lighter
filled with seawater
and carried it with me
as a stay against future glooms.

It's useless, this stranger said, pitying
my find, offering me a not badly
chipped sand-dollar I
didn't refuse, and

we diminished, each
to his way: I impoverished; he
picking over the particulate hardpack
with his heavy bag of agates all one color.

Invasives

High tide pressed me
up into
        the yellow, invasive
Scotch broom

whose roots hold fast this
crumbling cliff.

Against root-give, I clung
        ever more urgently to the *still*,
small voice — whose seeds

blew into me from 19c fields —
watching tankers drag

coal hillsides, tourist districts, shining decks
of cars past
        distant peaks,

and since this tide would not
retreat,
        cut a hard path up the cliff,
made my way through vacationers

sauntering the green of a fin de siècle
fort. Where genteel, sympathetic

                    murder was taught,
in haphazard rows,
children at art camp lounged with ice creams,

laughing avidly. There must be a real
higher or harder
than this, I said,
and took the trail up to a bluff overlooking
international waters,

            walked the rim of the impregnable
            concrete walls of the abandoned

gun emplacements. This is a place, finally,

nothing can invade,
I thought — admiring

            the Mayan-monumentality
            stripped

of phony deity —
I can build hard
                    apprehension here.

Up a narrow ladder, I climbed
            into the watchtower,

shut the iron visor, and
       sat in ammonia-smelling dark

where *deep* and *calm* and *perpetual*
could never take.

Then Japanese fire-balloons
                floated elegantly

past the long-range guns
in this afterimage

of a state-park plaque, touching down
70 years ago
        in Montana forests, igniting
        a recent candidate's promise

of colonies on the moon.

Out at the Root

Shore pine on the sea cliff,
perennial axletree on which
stars wheel — waves of the highest

high tide have half-unearthed
its hold. The intricate rootwork
that like sight of the covenant's ark

none should know, hangs exposed:
rainwashed, rope-thick roots scaffold
the vacancy where cliff was, and ends

of dangling rootlets, thread-thin,
pulse droplets like rosaries broken
continually. The upper canopy un-greens

needle by needle; the low notched
branch-ends interlock to gnash
in wind. Even its sudden hush is a harsh

suspension between constellation's cog
and log undressed by waves, ring by ring.
The immanence of no returning

deity inheres in its last distress.
It is a high unblessed separateness,
at last. At last, it is relentless.

Case Study

In the new buildings
are the old buildings;

in the old buildings
are the felled forests;

in the felled forests
are the forgotten verses;

in the forgotten verses
are the simple arrows

in glass cases
in the new buildings.

Note from Pergamon

The horses have trampled their legs to rubble.
The archer's hand floats free of his body at last.

Our glacial breasts have slipped down the precipice.
Rain softened our genitals to sorrowful marshland.

From our geometries, chimeras overcoming
earth. Serpents nurse on the grease of our axles.

Do not pity us, passenger on this
altar ship. You too are steered by a torso

whose thoughts are smoke of sacrifices.

Echolocation

These birds are called swallows, these clouds are called cumulus.
Grass grows straight from the roof of the small fortress.
In a film, the murdered ones water a garden.
The flies in the barracks have never heard of Terezín.

Swallow-flight ramifies through the small fortress.
The planks of the bunks don't recall any trees.
The flies in the barracks have never heard of me.
The lindens in rows once meant *hope for peace.*

The mirrors on the walls don't retain any face.
The human is distinguished by reflection and technology.
The lindens in rows once meant *execution-style.*
Guards swam under them in this empty pool.

The human is distinguished by language and memory.
Six thousand graves in rows under linden trees.
Guards peeled the dead up from sticky pools.
Some have said *dead*, others *exterminated*.

Six thousand shadows in rows under linden trees.
One can easily be confused by beauty.
Some have said *holocaust*, a word that means sacrifice.
A brown swallow on its nest inclines its head.

One can easily be confused by hope.
Some have claimed souls can come back as birds.
The prisoner on her knees inclined her head.
The code on the trains meant *No plan to return.*

Some have claimed souls can come back as beauty.
Sixty men in a room, standing in prayer.
The code on the trains meant *Someone remember me.*
A child stole bread and escaped in a movie.

Sixty men in a room, standing in piss.
My name means war in the language that authorized this.
A child stole bread and was shot in a movie.
I'm not among the murdered, but I feel I should pretend to be.

My name means war in a language that escapes me.
Last night I drank young Moravian wine.
I'm not among the murdered, why should I pretend to be?
The ashes of the bodies were dumped in this river.

Last night I drank *Coal-black milk of morning.*
Severed barbed wire hangs down here like nerves.
The names of the bodies were dumped in this river.
Many years later a man is fishing there.

Severed barbed wire hangs down here like vines.
In a film, the murdered ones water a garden.
Many years later a man is thinking there.
These birds are called *never*, these clouds are called *again*.

A Dish of Roman Nails

A clear glass dish of imperial noise;
of wood-and-plaster-wept ironic tears;
stripped pinnets of the augurs' foiled ploys;
creaking eyelashes of the brothel boys;
and prisoners' scratched-out years.

Who will return the spiders' obelisks,
re-order the teeth of the just decree,
discover again the geometers' styluses,
and calibrate the pleasure and the risk
of their breakneck traceries?

A nest of erections come to nothing,
monotonous notes of pounded praise,
full of the silence of — gravely opening
to witness the burdened elephant triumphing —
a thousand dismantled doorways.

A Door

Cities, streets, narrow to a door.
When you will arrive at it, how
it will transform what comes before
remains obscure. This is sure: it is

creaking near. The threshold
approaches to mute your feet
even as you sleep. I woke

in many cities: in Brooklyn woke
to lightning revealing a plot
of back-lot cornstalks: tall

as any door I'd ever seen.
I felt it seal the air. I could wake
all over earth, but I could not
hide this knock anywhere.

The Cloisters

Removed from pilgrimage routes,
reassembled across an ocean,
these arches once enclosed the spirit's orders
until death, and housed the bones.

Their placement now reflects, however mitigated
by curators' antiseptic fingers, a magnate's preference —
the rigors of the cross have been dispensed with,
and windows added facing the summer Hudson.

The Sunday crowd looks out, it shuffles through,
to see elsewhere the apse, the tapestries kept dark
preserving priceless gilts of cryptic dukes.
A dissected narwhale's horn offers proof
of the existence of the unicorn.

But linger under the rectilinear skylight
that protects from open air these courtyard walls,
and no fleshed-out relic of the word could seem enough
to take the walls again as limits of a life.

Instead a vision comes, of the vast pleasures left
to those freed from laying prayerful bedrock,
and in it, a Rockefeller sadly having his choice
of another stone head, in the purchasable world.

Sundress

This house crouches
under the others' porches.
Its driftwood-gray Victorian

scrollwork is ridiculous
when glimpsed in the total ambush
of rhododendron.

In the door, a narrow window is
hung for blind with a tie-dyed
dress, yellowish,

its sleeves pinned in alleluia position
to the frame's interior. The fashion
is forty years dead,

yet sunlight has so inhabited
the space hips belly and breasts once
lent dimension,

the dress seems to have been
hung here because
sunlight is

the size its wearer was.

Indivisible

She had been split already — twin
emerging after
an assertive sister;

split again
when one ear went dim
in a childhood disease;

split by early work,
her hands sweeping up
the bones bit clean by truckers
in the nightclub her father owned;

split by a church
that hung the naked beauty on the cross
and demanded that she cover up her knees.

Her growth was a meiosis reversed,
sloughing unnecessary halves

to consolidate the germ. She became
indivisible, the smallest nested doll

inside the parent shell
of a Dakota sky,

and then I split her
with my cries.

Note from an Ascendant Sect

We were told to plant nothing on the cliffs,
though no angel landed there ever.
When we went for water, some heard bleeding

behind the wall. Some saw the fluid coil
of the ram's horn repeated in the field's snakes,
and buried their vision in furrows — later, flowers

ensnared the corn. We couldn't hide
our nakedness from ourselves,
or stop hearing wings of skin descending

like brilliant rays of water, though we were told
our flesh was as a curtain
draping the eyes of our children

by that prophet who followed a trail
of textual keys to our corner of earth.
He left us suddenly, finding no

locked chests to open. Often,
two of us were met returning from the cliffs
with an upwelling secret.

A Certain Providence

Spiritualists, mediums, workers at the tripod table
with the one smaller leg, listeners
to mushrooms and handlers of amethyst,
astrologists, herbalists, ascenders
of volcanoes intermediary between earth and sky,
faces submerged in mineral bath or chemical trance,
alchemical midwives of the unborn elements,
I who have eaten bread every day of my life
and who still must ask if these are oat or wheat stalks
bending under their own heavy presence in no wind,
offer this my only certainty:

she lifted her yellow skirts to walk
a red-mud mountain road; her laugh
had that clarity there is no word for in any language
because understood openly by all;
she who had lived her entire life among crowds
walked the lost Silesian route of the salt and amber trade;
and I, who for years had languished
scholarly peaceful as Chuang Tzu's twisted stumps,
felt my fathers' wars rise in my name.

Magus

I pick the dandelion's
pointillist eye, blow it blind.

One astral capsule
fastens a spider's zodiac.

The spider, in
concentric meditation,

despite this
interpolation, is

undivided.
I am guided.

Calling

I could go credulous, could call
diminished sixths from the blanching chips
of a mouse's skull;

could take the rushes cased in ice
slow, slow, until the cases' tonic cracking
was fast below in nets of roots;

could loud, like the jay, rip shreds
of moss, richly dropletted, to incorporate
my vanishing;

could swell with the creek to cull
scribbled commandments from lowest branches — transient, yet
influencing the effluence;

could follow in deep leaf-muck
creek's meandering, and find unlooked-for terns'
green deafening. I sat then,

incredulous, in colors beyond calling, sat
until I picked from the din the heron's eye
that transforms

low fish-bones into long, silent flight.

Note from the Etruscans

When you are finally alone, the canopy of your wings
will drape over you, the stream will run through
the comb of your bones without straightening,
and the shadows of your breasts will be kept in shallow bowls.

If you missed the path where the seedpods stop rattling,
your necklace will have to be slipped off and lost
before you can wade into the silence

of a simple handle dropped in a field,
before you can know a wheel turned on its side
is a round of contentment to confound the clouds.

Even then you will find your eyes are stylized olives
painted on a slate, that have never actually opened,
and your mouth opened to sing is full of seeds rattling.
Then your whole body will slip through your ring.

Tired of Explaining Seasons to the Sun,

I on the mountain descended
        below the clouds, to overturn loose slates
on the black stream's rubble bottom.

I picked from the first slate an elegant utterance,
        a caddisfly's woven pebble cone
stitched with nearly invisible spicules
        to its obscure stone roof,
and peeled the pebble cone to see

        the appalled pupa
filtering specks of plant-matter
into pulpy, papery wings,
        to smuggle them clumsily
        to the stream's surface someday

(to float in total vulnerability
to cutthroat trout, common sparrows,
streamside webs), waiting for the sun to dry them

that it might clobber and climb a mate
        in air, completing its pattern no closer to the sun
than tips of shoreline scrub;

        but in peeling, I
        split the soft wing-sac
        with a barbed thumb.

There was no repairing
        the plucked one unpearling
in my palm, so I begged the flashing trout-mouths
return this

and climbed a rise above the stream scooped sheer
        by an eddy's clockwise coil,
        parted thick weeds, and peered
into the coil's center:

a thousand tinier spindles of spring-water unwound
long strands of silt,
        and muscular shapes, suspended
against the loose ends, flicked livid tails
        over a seam of bluish alluvium.

        I dripped the sticky pupa
        from the thumb-tip
        into stream's pupil.

The mouths blinked wildly,
clouds broke behind me, making the water mirror
        my crouching form, revealing the sun
        crouching over me.

I turned, scrambled back from the rise, and was
     snared by a strand of nettles;
     barbed weed split my lip,
     ground knocked the seasons out of me,
and leaves disguised as never fallen seethed:

return this return this.

October

for John Keats and Nick Drake

Autumnals overheard
in the next room, I have passed the place
where you turned back.

The loaded apple boughs are there,
color unchanging; a sound repeats

your second grace forever.
I drive on, into late corn, find everywhere
wide paths cut for cables

that feed the alien screens.
On one screen I saw shining husks rustle

with your words in the chill
celibacy that has crept backward
over your lives. This room is smallest.

The corn of Ruth, even, is gone.

Preserve

A tall animal has printed the snow drift
on this pond's ice roof.
Incautious to the risk of falling through,
it has crossed. Emerson

assured a version of me more integral
awaits my determination to meet it
in woods. He uses me

to meet himself in woods in me.
On the shoreline, through shafts in the snow crust:
cleft hoof prints, frail blue.

Deer or devil, this creature
walks ungingerly, drops scat freely, peels long strips
of bark from the oldest trees, and the trace
its walking makes — doubling and redoubling,
impossible to follow — makes
its way its way.

I stand in dense saplings the hoof prints have split
to cross the pond. Will I find I wait for me
on that other side, or find Emerson only
an echo

diminished to this preserve?
Such a thin roof of ice upholds such wondering.
It shakes and crazes in the human thunders
of planes in descent to O'Hare.

I stand out under the evaporating banners
of others' journeys — earth is rapidly less than actual
size.

Trace I read in the snow, you are wise.
I must be otherwise.

After Hopkins

Indivisble I divine
　　　　in leaf's veins, lung's blood,
　　　　　　　floodplain, and feathered cloud,
where the all ails, avail.

We've summoned by reduction
　　　　the valenced none, digressed,
　　　　　　　through manias of distinction,
out of reverence, are undeceived

and undone. Therefore, repair.
　　　　Let mountain and meteorite
　　　　　　　accord in scale, write in alleles
aves in human and bacterium alike.

Let us learn to lean again
　　　　on the awe-obstinate phrase,
　　　　　　　like that poor priest who fused
the disparate trout spots,

　　　　　　　cloud colors, into one praise.

Acknowledgements

Grateful acknowledgement is due to the editors of the journals where versions of some of these poems first appeared:

32 Poems: "Sundress"
American Letters and Commentary: "A Door"
Antioch Review: "Echolocation"
Cincinnati Review: "Note from Pergamon"
Commonweal: "After Hopkins," "Out at the Root"
Conjunctions (Web): "I, Inc."
CutBank: "Falstaff Sifting Fish Trash," "The End of Metaphor"
DIAGRAM: "Invasives"
Faultline: "Discovery Park," "Fallen Empire's Tiny Chemical Sun"
Inscape: "Astral Plaint"
The Iowa Review: "Note from an Ascendant Sect," "Note from the Etruscans"
Iron Horse Literary Review: "Combers"
The Journal: "Magus"
Likestarlings: "Compass," "Conditions of Blood," "Fishing Rock"
Mare Nostrum: "A Dish of Roman Nails"
Midwest Quarterly: "Hinoki"
Minnetonka Review: "Inversion between the Fish Counters at Bonneville Dam," "Outskirts," "The Cloisters"
North American Review: "Preserve"
North Dakota Quarterly: "Domus Aurea," "Speck"
Notre Dame Review: "Levels"
Poet Lore: "Atlas Industries"
Portland Review: "Note from the Romans"
Roanoke Review: "Indivisible"
Seneca Review: "Case Study," "Tired of Explaining Seasons to the Sun,"
Shenandoah: "Calling"
South Dakota Review: "Clasp," "Fraught Stop on the Coast," "Sweet Delay," "Standstill"
Sou'wester: "Processed"
The Spoon River Poetry Review: "November"

Some of these poems were collected in *Source to Mouth*, a chapbook published by New Michigan Press. "Magus" was reprinted in *Verse Daily*.

"Coal-black milk of morning" is taken from Donald White's translation of Paul Celan's poem "Todesfuge."

About the Author

Brandon Krieg grew up in Tualatin, Oregon, and attended Cornell University, The University of Washington, and Western Michigan University. He is the author of a chapbook, Source to Mouth (New Michigan Press), and his poems have appeared in *Conjunctions*, *The Iowa Review*, *Antioch Review*, and many other journals. He is a founding editor of *The Winter Anthology* (www.winteranthology. com) and an associate editor of *Poetry Northwest*. He lives in Kalamazoo, Michigan, with his wife, Colleen O'Brien, and their son, Ezra.

About New Rivers Press

New Rivers Press emerged from a drafty Massachusetts barn in winter 1968. Intent on publishing work by new and emerging poets, founder C. W. "Bill" Truesdale labored for weeks over an old Chandler & Price letterpress to publish three hundred fifty copies of Margaret Randall's collection, *So Many Rooms Has a House But One Roof*.

Nearly four hundred titles later, New Rivers, a non-profit and now teaching press based since 2001 at Minnesota State University Moorhead, has remained true to Bill's goal of publishing the best new literature — poetry and prose — from new, emerging, and established writers.

New Rivers Press authors range in age from twenty to eighty-nine. They include a silversmith, a carpenter, a geneticist, a monk, a tree-trimmer, and a rock musician. They hail from cities such as Christchurch, Honolulu, New Orleans, New York City, Northfield (Minnesota), and Prague.

Charles Baxter, one of the first authors with New Rivers, calls the press "the hidden backbone of the American literary tradition." Continuing this tradition, in 1981 New Rivers began to sponsor the Minnesota Voices Project — now called Many Voices Project — competition. It is one of the oldest literary competitions in the United States, bringing recognition and attention to emerging writers. Other New Rivers publications include the American Fiction Series, the American Poetry Series, New Rivers Abroad, and the Electronic Book Series.

We invite you to visit our website, newriverspress.com, for more information.

Many Voices Project Award Winners

"OP" indicates that the paper copy is out of print; "e-book" indicates that the title is available as an electronic publication.

130 *Dispensations*, Randolph Thomas (e-book)

129 *Invasives*, Brandon Krieg

128 *Whitney*, Joe Stracci (e-book)

127 *Rare Earth*, Bradford Tice

126 *The Way of All Flux*, Sharon Suzuki-Martinez

125 *It Takes You Over*, Nick Healy (e-book)

124 *The Muse of Ocean Parkway and Other Stories*, Jacob Lampart (e-book)

123 *Hotel Utopia*, Robert Miltner

122 *Kinesthesia*, Stephanie N. Johnson

121 *Birds of Wisconsin*, B.J. Best

120 *At Home Anywhere*, Mary Hoffman (e-book)

119 *Friend Among Stones*, Maya Pindyck

118 *Fallibility*, Elizabeth Oness

117 *When Love Was Clean Underwear*, Susan Barr-Toman (e-book)

116 *The Sound of It*, Tim Nolan

115 *Hollow Out*, Kelsea Habecker

114 *Bend from the Knees*, Benjamin Drevlow

113 *The Tender, Wild Things*, Diane Jarvenpa

112 *Signaling for Rescue*, Marianne Herrmann

111 *Cars Go Fast*, John Chattin

110 *Terrain Tracks*, Purvi Shah

109 *Numerology and Other Stories*, Christian Michener

108 *Not a Matter of Love*, Beth Alvarado (e-book)

107 *Real Karaoke People*, Ed Bok Lee

106 *Love in An Expanding Universe*, Ron Rindo